Have you ever watched one of my videos?

This is my family. I live with my mommy, my daddy, and my sisters. My family appears in a lot of my videos!

This is my mommy. She used to be a high school science teacher, but now we make videos together.

She's really funny in front of the camera and doesn't get nervous!

This is my daddy. My daddy used to be a structural engineer. He helped design and build buildings. My daddy is a little shy in front of the camera, but we always have a lot of fun anyway!

These are my little sisters, Emma and Kate. They're twins, which means they were born on the same day. Many people think my sisters look alike, but I never have any trouble telling them apart. Emma and Kate are two years old, and they always have a lot of energy! They also started their own animated YouTube channel, called EK Doodles.

I love being a big brother. It is so much fun to play with my sisters, especially chase and hide-and-seek. Do you have any siblings?

Now that you've met my family, let me tell you all about my videos. I've been posting on my YouTube channel Ryan ToysReview since I was three.

I have a Silver Play Button trophy from when I got one hundred thousand subscribers and a Gold Play Button trophy from when I got 1 million subscribers. I also have a Diamond Play Button for 10 million subscribers!

Lots of my videos are about toys. I love playing with toys. My favorites are LEGO blocks and action figures. What are your favorite toys?

In my videos, I sometimes unbox toys. Or I find them inside surprise eggs. One time I even dove into a pool of Orbeez to look for them! It's so exciting when I open up a new toy!

But I don't just make videos about toys. I post all kinds of videos on my channel. I like making music videos. I sing nursery rhymes and holiday songs. I like to dance when I sing.

Do you like music? I love it. I go to a music class where I play the drums, guitar, shakers, and keyboard. Learning about music and playing it is a lot of fun!

You can learn a lot of cool facts from my science videos. For example, did you know that the biggest shark is the whale shark? It can grow to more than forty feet—about as long as a school bus!

I do science experiments on my channel too.

What happens when you mix baking soda and vinegar? What about Mentos and Diet Coke? You'll have to watch my videos to find out!

I also have a gaming channel called VTubers. I made it because I love playing video games and watching other people play them on YouTube.

My mommy, my daddy, and I play all kinds of games. We have a special gaming room with everything you need for gaming: a giant computer, a TV, a Wii U, a PlayStation 4, and more! My favorite game is *Roblox*. What's yours?

I love gaming so much that I want to be a game developer when I grow up. Then I can spend all day making video games! Or maybe I'll be a video editor and make cool videos. Of course, I hope I'm still making YouTube videos when I'm older.

One of the best parts of being on YouTube is my fans! It makes me so happy when fans tell me that they watch my videos. Once a fan came up to me and said, "How are you here? I saw you on my iPad!" That was funny. You might watch me on your screen, but in real life, I'm just a regular kid like you!

Sometimes I meet fans on the playground. I like it when kids say hi because I feel like I have a new friend . . . and I love making new friends!

Thanks for reading all about me! I hope to see you on my channel someday!

Meet Ryan's friends from  RYAN'S WORLD™ !

Did you know Ryan can transform into a superhero? **Red Titan** is superstrong. He can lift anything and break through walls. *Kapow!*

Combo Panda loves gaming. You can catch him playing on VTubers and on his own YouTube channel. Combo Crew, here we go—it's showtime!

Big Gil plays video games from his cozy underwater room. Whether he's running around on *Roblox* or racing on *Mario kart*, Gil is never afraid to show off his "gil skills"!

Peck the penguin hails from the South Pole. He loves Popsicles and wants to become a gr scientist someday.

Alpha Lexa is a gamer girl with a passion for fashion. She'll stop at nothing to win a game!

Gus the Gummy Gator li going on wild adventures But there's one thing he likes more than anything else—yummy gummies!

Moe is from Moetopia, a farawa planet. He likes building with toys and joining Gus on his adventures.

Come visit Ryan and his friends on his YouTube channel!
www.youtube.com/ryantoysreview

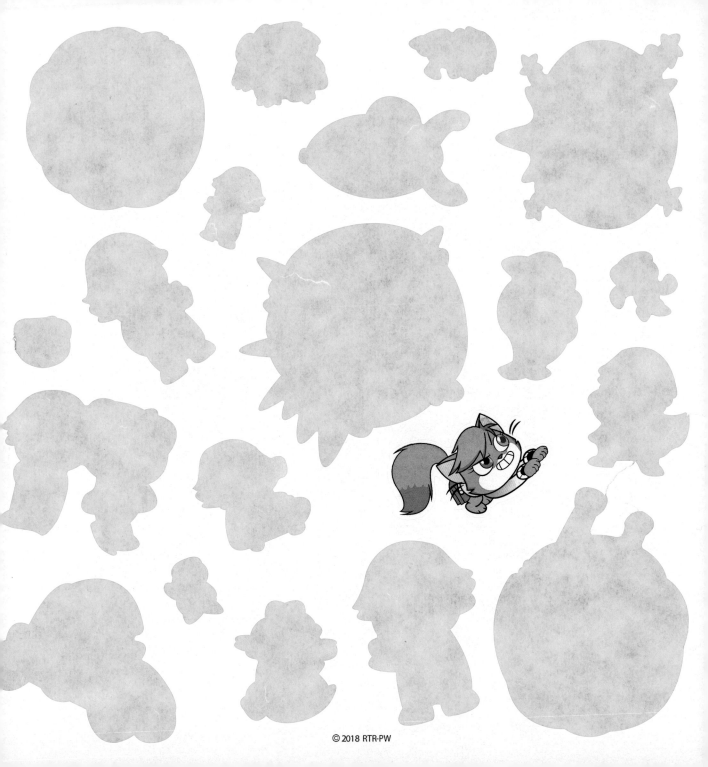